RETAIL THERAPY

STORE DESIGN TODAY

RETAIL THERAPY

STORE DESIGN TODAY

Edited by Andrea Boekel

images
Publishing

Published in Australia in 2007 by
The Images Publishing Group Pty Ltd
ABN 89 059 734 431
6 Bastow Place, Mulgrave, Victoria 3170, Australia
Tel: +61 3 9561 5544 Fax: +61 3 9561 4860
books@imagespublishing.com
www.imagespublishing.com

Copyright © The Images Publishing Group Pty Ltd 2007
The Images Publishing Group Reference Number: 716

National Library of Australia Cataloguing-in-Publication entry:

Retail Therapy.

ISBN 9 781864701159

1. Stores, Retail – Designs and plans. 2. Public architecture. 3. Urban
landscape architecture. 4. Public spaces. I. Boekel, Andrea

725.21

Edited by Andrea Boekel

Designed by The Graphic Image Studio Pty Ltd, Mulgrave, Australia
www.tgis.com.au

Digital production by Splitting Image Colour Studio Pty Ltd, Australia

Printed by Sing Cheong Printing Co. Ltd. Hong Kong

IMAGES has included on its website a page for special notices in relation to
this and our other publications. Please visit www.imagespublishing.com

CONTENTS

Miss Sixty
South Coast Plaza, California, USA
Giorgio Borruso Design

1   Suspended cocoon-shaped dressing rooms made of special ultra-light aluminium circles surrounded with stretchy translucent fabric have a distinct avant-garde feel
2   The approach to the store is an oversized metal sculptural element surrounded by glass. The stainless steel polished mirror door has 12 conical portholes
3   The portholes represent the perfect result of geometric calculation utilising regular elements such as the rectangle and circle: symbols of symmetry, order and simplicity
4   Curved ceiling drops down and returns to original height at back where grouping of cocoons is suspended. Natural daylight enters from large window
5   Detail of polished mirror door

Photography: Benny Chan

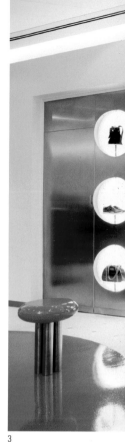

1

3

2

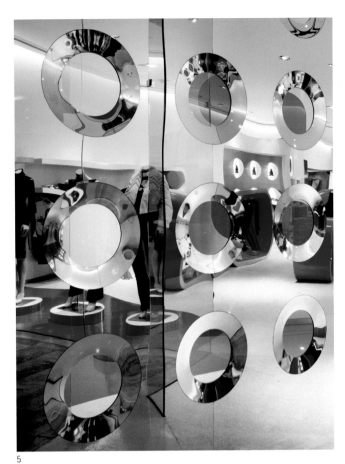

Miss Sixty
South Coast Plaza, California, USA
Giorgio Borruso Design

6   Interior of this store retailing high-end Italian line of jeans, clothes and accessories consists of simple forms, circles and squares

7   1960's Panton style is seen in curves that become more complex when reflected in floors and ceiling

8   Cocoon-style changing rooms of varying diameters are free-standing

Photography: Benny Chan

7

Vaughan Mills
Vaughan, Ontario, Canada
Executive Architect: Bregman + Hamann Architects
Design Architect: JPRA Architects

1 This centre is divided into six unique neighbourhoods based on the design theme 'Discover Ontario'
2 Striking signage at one of the entry points to the centre
3 Modern illuminated sculptures adorn neighbourhood entrances

Photography: richardjohnson.ca

2

3

Vaughan Mills
Vaughan, Ontario, Canada
Executive Architect:
Bregman + Hamann Architects
Design Architect: JPRA Architects

4–7 One of the largest shopping and entertainment centres in the region, Vaughan Mills boasts more than 200 speciality shops, restaurants and entertainment venues

Photography: richardjohnson.ca

4

6

1

2

3

4

Bjorn Eyewear 1
San Francisco, California, USA
Taylor Fierce Architects, Inc

1   Polished wooden floors and counters add a touch of warmth
2   Eyewear displays are consumer-friendly
3   Store is located in a second-floor walkway space on Union Street
4   Design of this flagship store is seen as an integral part of the branding effort for a national expansion

Photography: courtesy Taylor Fierce Architects, Inc

Fornarina
Via Cola di Rienzo, Rome, Italy
Giorgio Borruso Design

1   Focal point of the store is the black, tree-like central element that penetrates the ceiling and liquefies into the floor, contrasting with the sleek whiteness
2   Chrome rings displaying precious objects extend from the tree towards the entry
3   Singular eye on the black tree-like structure seems to watch over the customers
Photography: Benny Chan

2

3

1

2

3

5

6

7

ILVA Malmø
Malmø, Sweden
schmidt hammer lassen k/s

1   The first ILVA store outside Denmark, centrally situated in the Øresund region, its rectangular volume has an open main façade overlooking the arrival and parking area

2&3 Café and registers are part of the design scheme

4   Strong daylight entering from overhead is a special feature of the display area

5&6 Other spatial experiences combine with the furniture displays: a softly lit bed area and an open, closely packed furnishing accessories department

7   A distinctive stairway connects the two storeys

Photography: courtesy ILVA

Queens Quay Terminal
Toronto, Ontario, Canada
Zeidler Partnership Architects

1 Overlooking Toronto's harbourfront, a former storage facility is transformed into an active, year-round, mixed-use project

2&3 Interior views of retail levels; this unique conversion was recently chosen as being among the most important architecture of the 20th century in Canada by *Canada Architect* magazine

Photography: Fiona Spalding-Smith

1

Megastore Auchan Bielany
Bielany, Wroclaw, Poland
Ozone Studio Architektoniczne

1&2 Unique style of lighting provides
warmth to the interiors while
flooring design complements
the overall store layout

Photography: courtesy Ozone Studio Architektoniczne

Auchan Moscow Marfino
Moscow, Russia
Ozone Studio Architektoniczne

3&4 The third Auchan megastore in
Moscow deviated from its usual
'hut' type character. New colours
and materials were used. Photographs
of people in spontaneous poses
created an impression of chaos.

Photography: courtesy Ozone Studio Architektoniczne

b.open
Bielany, Wroclaw, Poland
Ozone Studio Architektoniczne

5&6 Design concept of store uses modern
materials and specific lighting resulting
in a trendy look

Photography: courtesy Ozone Studio Architektoniczne

1

2

3

4

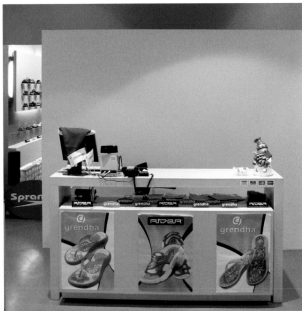

5

6

Madame Suren
Omaha, Nebraska, USA
Randy Brown Architects

Opposite:
   This 'Soho-type' boutique opened by two innovative women showcases unique clothing and accessories that cannot be found elsewhere in this Midwestern city
2   Unfinished concrete floors and exposed ceilings create a sleek, minimal backdrop to the displays
3   Light wall at back of store envelops it in a white glow in the evening
Photography: Farshid Assassi

2

3

Klara Zenit
Stockholm, Sweden
Equator AB Stockholm

1 Debenham's warm inviting entrance faces a pedestrian walk. Stone and glass are bathed in light.
2 Generous double-height entrance characterises department store entrance facing Drottninggatan. Entrance delineates border between retail and offices. View towards landmark office tower.

Opposite:
Located on Stockholm's main shopping walk, Drottninggatan, Klara Zenit has attracted many high-profile tenants including chains Debenhams and H & M

Photography: Max Plunger

1

Scissors' Hands Hairdressing & Beauty Centre
Akatlar, Istanbul, Turkey
Habif Mimarlik Insaat Ticaret A.S
1   Horizontal and vertical surfaces combine mosaic, stone, wood and glass in perfect harmony
2&3   Centre was created by redecorating an independent villa
4   The male barber is located on the ground floor and the female hairdressing area is on the first floor
Photography: Gurkan Akay

2

3

4

Scissors' Hands Hairdressing & Beauty Centre
Akatlar, Istanbul, Turkey
Habif Mimarlik Insaat Ticaret A.S

5   Modern décor provides perfect conditions for the youthful and energetic staff
6&7   Male and female sections are clearly delineated
8   Soft lighting combines with natural materials to create a warm, welcoming feel

Photography: Gurkan Akay

6

5

7

8

The Turner Store at CNN Center
Atlanta, Georgia, USA
ASD/sky design
1   Front of store has fresh and exciting identity that interacts with visitors
2   View of new ticket kiosk at the start of the 'Inside CNN' tour
3   Glass at rear of store captures visitors' attention
Photography: Robbins Photography

2

3

The Turner Store at CNN Center
Atlanta, Georgia, USA
ASD/sky design

4   Environmental graphics are used to represent
    CNN brand throughout the store and tour
5   Store interior with customised retail display,
    lighting and messaging systems
6   Cartoon figures and their surroundings come
    to life as the backdrop for merchandise

Photography: Robbins Photography

4

Grafic
Woodbridge, Ontario, Canada
Johnson Chou Inc

1   Entry into this elegant menswear boutique is through a tube-like form that is an extrusion of the
storefront glass. This structure defines the cash area and initiates the processional sequence.

2&3   Design concept creates an assemblage of discrete objects activated and linked by movement

Photography: Volker Seding

1

2

3

Chevy Chase Center
Chevy Chase, Maryland, USA
HOK

1 Curve of Wisconsin Circle is followed in the eight-storey office tower's glass and precast façades and the interior design of the main entry lobby

2 Granite sculptures and a serene water feature enliven a part of the space

3&5 Enhancements to streetscape, which include increased sidewalk widths, speciality lighting and landscaping, help to define the space and character of Wisconsin Avenue and contribute to the vibrancy of the area

4 This centre replaced a 50-year-old suburban strip shopping centre, low-rise office building and large surface strip parking lot

6&7 Nestled between the two buildings of the shopping centre is a public space designed as a respite from the main thoroughfare

Photography: Joseph Romeo

1

2

3

4

5

6

7

Walgreens at Views @ 270
Hollywood, California, USA
M2A Milofsky Michali & Cox Architects

8   Popular chainstore Walgreens is located on the ground floor of a 56-unit housing development. An adult theatre and derelict stores blighted this quarter along fabled Sunset Boulevard in Hollywood but today, maintains the urban street edge and reinforces the vitality of the adjoining pedestrian environment

Photography: Tom Bonner Photography

8

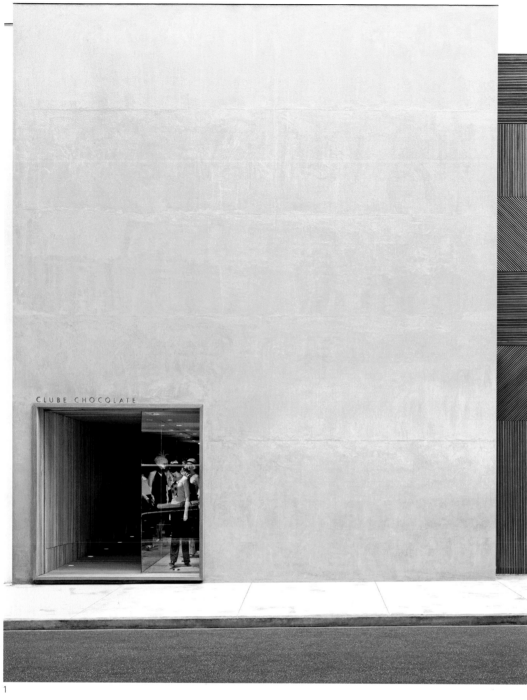

1

2

3

Clube Chocolate
São Paulo, Brazil
Isay Weinfeld
1   Discreet entry to this shop and gallery belies the merchandise within
2   Display of renowned national and international fashions for men and women
3   A cosy café and upscale martini bar are part of the Clube Chocolate concept
Photography: Alvaro Póvoa and Tuca Reinés

4

5

Clube Chocolate
São Paulo, Brazil
Isay Weinfeld

4 This store's concept offers a variety of unexpected delights that does not quite fit neatly into any shopping category
5 A variety of merchandise including plants, gift items and homewares is displayed
6 General view of store through void with spiral stairway in background
7 Interestingly, 'Chocolate' is a Brazilian clothing label displayed among the other items of merchandise
8 Spiral stairway to the upper level

Photography: Alvaro Póvoa and Tuca Reinés

8

Kult
Berlin, Germany
Corneille Uedingslohmann Architekten

1   Area for products on sale with a flagstone wall behind
2   Display shelves are illuminated and provide a special effect
3   Detail of display rack
4   Work island with coat rack above
Photography: Joachim Wagner

1

3

4

Kult
Berlin, Germany
Corneille Uedingslohmann Architekten

5   Wooden island with clothing displays
6   Illuminated shelves with work station
     beyond
7   Unique display solutions offer interesting
     methods of showcasing apparel
8   Freestanding displays on high-gloss floors
     impart a touch of luxury

Photography: Joachim Wagner

5

7

l.a. Eyeworks
Los Angeles, California, USA
Neil M. Denari Architects

1   Beverly Boulevard front is sleek and elegant
2   Wall by notable designer is perfect
    background for product displays
Opposite:
    Glass detail on front window
Photography: Neil M. Denari

1

l.a. Eyeworks
Los Angeles, California, USA
Neil M. Denari Architects

4   Interesting Isermann wall has a three-dimensional effect
5   View from entry door. Gaseous blue interior and subtle lighting
     provide cool and restful ambience.

Photography: Neil M. Denari

5

Axel Springer Headquarters
Berlin, Germany
RHWL Architects

1   Convenience shops, restaurants and a classy bar sit under individual umbrellas formed by glass domes in the public space of Europe's biggest publishing house. Main entrance at Markgraffenstrasse is bustling with activity.
2   At lunch time, courtyard cafés are filled with customers
3   Public space is a sequence of glass-covered courtyards and passages and the light and airy atmosphere created is indicative of the traditional Berlin 'hof'. Double-volume passages connect all courtyards.
4   'Deli News' is one of several restaurants in passage
5   Central 'Mittelbar' features aquariums and integrated projection screens
6   Lush bamboo in granite planter boxes that double up as benches
Photography: © Stefan Muller

3

1

4

5

6

1

2

3

s.Oliver Store
Munich, Germany
plajer & franz studio

1&2 Bright red signage represents the familiar and highly respected s.Oliver stores concept
  3 Suspended gypsum board ceiling with chrome laminate is offset by red lamellae
      featured throughout the store

Photography: diephotodesigner.de

s.Oliver Store
Munich, Germany
plajer & franz studio

4   'Anastacia by s.Oliver' – positive message of the popular singer is displayed by the shop concept. The tattoo is a recurring decorative element while large images and screens showing current video clips of Anastacia are arranged on the back wall
5   s.Oliver Casual Woman underlines a modern look with its subtle red and white appearance
6   Jeans are presented in both hung and stacked displays
7   Vertical and horizontal lamellae elements underline the modern look of the casual women's wear section

Photography: diephotodesigner.de

5

6

7

s.Oliver Store
Munich, Germany
plajer & franz studio

8   Menswear section is sleek and sophisticated with mirrored ceilings and discreet seating

9   Blue accents on mirrored ceiling and dark floor tiles make the formal menswear area inviting

10 Accessories division with its crisp red and white colour scheme

11 Free-standing displays are customer friendly and offer a feeling of uncluttered elegance

Photography: diephotodesigner.de

8

s.Oliver Store
Munich, Germany
plajer & franz studio

12&14   Seating outside changing rooms is a unique feature of the store

13   In the SELECTION women's section, dark floor tiles are juxtaposed with the chrome laminate ceiling, walls are covered with silver striped wallpaper and round Macassar ebony tables lacquered in white and beige set refined accents

15   s.Oliver BODYWEAR is clearly aligned with the other sections, creating a perfect connection for the lingerie product displays. Wallpaper is silver and aubergine with pink plush carpet and gauze curtains.

Photography: diephotodesigner.de

12

13

16

18

19

ge 2 to 6 size 92 to 128

s.Oliver Store
Munich, Germany
plajer & franz studio

16   Juniors sections have a green colour scheme for the boys and pink for the girls

17   Simulated dalmatian fur display units add a playful element

18   Overhead signage promotes branding

19   Backlit ceiling elements in combination with a series of circular fluorescent tubes
        create beautiful lighting within the space

Photography: diephotodesigner.de

Giuseppe Zanotti Design
Las Vegas, Nevada, USA
ICRAVE Design Studio

1   Three large custom-designed resin rings pivot to become window displays when the store is closed
2   Unique wedge-shaped floor plan allows for a seamless entry from the mall concourse
3   Guiseppe Zanotti's sexy and playful footwear designs inspired the fresh design approach to this store
4   Resin pedestals display shoes as artwork evoking the feeling of luxury

Photography: courtesy ICRAVE Design

1

2

3

4

Giuseppe Zanotti Design
Las Vegas, Nevada, USA
ICRAVE Design Studio
5   Glass bubble chandelier is suspended over a large, circular banquette that provides comfortable seating
6   Curved and slanted wall is constructed from shiny zinc panels, creating the feel of a glamorous marquee
Photography: courtesy ICRAVE Design

5

6

SnAKS at Paris Fashion Archive
New York, New York, USA
II BY II Design Associates Inc.

1   International furniture by Warren Platner upholstered with lavender wool
    says it echoes a design icon of the modern era.

2   A glass is presented from women's shoe department by large chrome wires
    are frosted and clear acrylic tubes. An oversized black-and-white photo of
    Paris Montana's glamourous muse, Rosie de Palma adorns the wall.

3   Each screen's reflective floor is textured with small discs to create special
    reflections. The bar's polished surface and bar stool seats are covered
    with white leather.

4– Thin, single trumpet forms, chrome-edged white glass table tops feature
    discreet tile red piano floors.

Photographs: Ben Rahnik-Hone Inc.

1

3

4

5

6

1

2

3

1   Fairy tale of Little Red Riding Hood and
    the evil wolf is the inspiration behind this
    store that retails fashion, accessories,
    literature and music relating to Grimm's
    fairy tales. Ground-floor entrance from
    Friedrichstrasse
2   Superb lighting highlights gloss finish of
    display shelves
3   Panoramic view of basement and its
    merchandise displays

Photography: Joachim Wagner

4

LITTL
E
RED
RIDIN
G
HOO
D_

5

6

7

Little Red Riding Hood Shop
Berlin, Germany
Corneille Uedingslohmann Architekten

4 View of basement with its interesting product display stands
5 Unique signage announcing store
6&8 Product display
7 View from basement up to projection screen on ground level

Photography: Joachim Wagner

8

1

3

Madrid Xanadu
Madrid, Spain
Commarts Design

1   Home to the first Snow Dome in southern Europe – an enormous indoor, year-round slope with 100 vertical metres and a run of nearly 1 kilometre, this centre skilfully combines the retail and entertainment experience

2&4 Use of light and strong animated forms of calligraphic tubing 'canopies' bring the scale and volume down to that of the people

3   Environmental graphics, colour palettes and furniture combine as characters in space to animate and engage the visitor

Photography: Henry Beer, Communication Arts Inc.

4

Southside Central Shopping Centre
Bundaberg, Queensland, Australia
PDT Architects

1   Speciality shops off car park
2   Supermarket entrance portico
3   Speciality shops entry

Photography: Graham Meltzer Architectural Photography

Gallery at Harborplace
Baltimore, Maryland, USA
Zeidler Partnership Architects

4   Red granite base and glass and metal cladding blend with colours of nearby buildings
5   A linear sequence of escalators leads up the four-storey retail atrium

Photography: Balthazar Korab

1

2

3

4

5

The Mall at Millenia
Orlando, Florida, USA
JPRA Architects

1   Water garden entrance. Palm trees lit from below add vertical symmetry.
2   View of lower level through Grand Court towards mall
3   Water garden interior with fountain and elevators
4   Second level of mall with Juliet balcony

Photography: Tom Hurst Photography

3

4

The Mall at Millenia
Orlando, Florida, USA
JPRA Architects

5   Orangerie café restaurants and dining
    area
6   Upper-level view to Grand Court
7   Winter garden upper-level entrance
8   View of Orchid Court from upper level
Photography: Tom Hurst Photography

5

6

7

1

2

**+ IT Fashion
Cannes, France
BARTOLINI\LANZI architects**

1 Inside view: white resin floor, ceiling and walls frame coloured displays

2 All display niches are surrounded by indirect lighting while general lighting is recessed

3 Displays face each other at the back of store; Zen garden is visible from the window

4 Three fitting rooms are covered with staggered mirrors

Photography: Alessandro Bartolini

3

4

Bjorn Eyewear 2
San Francisco, California, USA
Taylor Fierce Architects, Inc.

1 Entry from street
2 Interesting lighting systems offer maximum exposure to products displayed
3 The second store for Bjorn Eyewear is located on the ground floor of an existing brick masonry building and looks out to Market Street in the Castro neighbourhood
4 Interior of store is airy and spacious with informal product displays

Photography: courtesy Taylor Fierce Architects, Inc.

1

2

3

4

Acne Jeans Store
Berlin, Germany
Gonzalez / Haase Atelier Architecture & Scenography

1   For the first store outside Scandinavia of hip Swedish brand of jeans, the design was based on a technique devised from 3D modelling software
2   Light installation reminiscent of a pair of antlers generates a white, luminous fixture in the ceiling
3   Minimalist displays are in keeping with the store's ultra-modern concept

Photography: Thomas Meyer/Ostkreuz

1

2

1

2

etre belle Kiosk
Toronto, Ontario, Canada
Bregman + Hamann Architects

1 This cosmetic kiosk was a prototype design for locations across North America

2 Kiosk promotes advanced skincare technology methods and uses clean curvilinear forms that use light and innovative displays to highlight the product

3&4 Kiosk was installed at the Hudson Bay Company's flagship Queen and Yonge Street store and promoted a high-end European cosmetic company

Photography: Kerun Ip

3

4

1

2

Colour Bar
Prospect, South Australia, Australia
Studio 9 Architects Pty Ltd

1 Clever architectural elements, shapes and spaces, with a transparent yet strong frontage, draw clientele into the shop from the shopping centre mall. A coffee bar in the waiting area attracts passing clientele.

2 Practical planning and innovative fitouts increased the accommodation in the shop

3 Shop invents a new and exciting retail image and store concept for emerging Colour Bar hairdressing chain. Kit of parts concept and corporate identity such as the pods and components can be applied to other new situations.

4 By reinventing the nature of some hair salon working spaces to form new shapes and working relationships, it was possible to overcome the spatial limitations

5 Working areas are open and spacious with large mirrors and good storage spaces

Photography: Sarah Long Photography

3

4

5

1

Somerset Collection South Renovation
Troy, Michigan, USA
JPRA Architects
1   Main entry rotunda and concierge. Light filtering in from
    glass dome throws ethereal glow on tiled floor below.
2   Centre court fountain, glass art and hardscape details
3   Centre court sculpture and art glass details
Photography: Tom Hurst Photography

2

3

**Somerset Collection South Renovation
Troy, Michigan, USA**
JPRA Architects

4   Glass elevator and fountain; violet-coloured
    blossoms add a chic touch
5   Centre court with its glass sculptures, hard paved
    areas and plants bring a touch of the outside in

Photography: Tom Hurst Photography

4

Olymp & Hades
Stuttgart, Germany
Corneille Uedingslohmann Architekten

1   First floor mall entrance
2   Display section with its upturned dome-
    like display stands
3   Changing rooms
4   Innovative display racks present products
    in unique style
5   Dome-like theme follows through in
    overhead lighting fixtures and display
    pedestals

Photography: Joachim Wagner

1

2

3

4

5

Olymp & Hades
Stuttgart, Germany
Corneille Uedingslohmann Architekten

6   Cash desk and reception
7   Menswear display
8&10   Mall entry from first floor
9   Unique display wall
Photography: Joachim Wagner

6

8

9

10

Attachment Boutique
Shibuya, Tokyo, Japan
Area Design

1 View of store entrance at night
2 Interior of store, with its cool, muted ambience provides ideal environment for customers

Photography: Daici Ano

1

2

1

Habitat
Dublin, Ireland
Mellett Architects

1   The store occupies the banking hall of 18th-century Bank of Ireland building, and 1960's office building

2   Majestic banking hall was restored with a new floating restaurant gently inserted within

3   Historic colour palettes have been used as a tribute to past architectural triumphs

Photography: courtesy Mellett Architects

2

3

1

2

1 In the heart of Mitte, Berlin, this small boutique is at the crossroads of several busy streets and is triangular-shaped in keeping with the outside perspective

2 The design is deceptive and not quite in keeping with that of a lingerie boutique

3 Large, glossy monolithic furniture in monochrome neutral grey gleams under light and contrasts with the untreated oak floor

4 Large cabinet display has boxed lingerie as if in an archive store

Photography: Thomas Meyer/Ostkreuz

3

4

1

2

3

Lorenzetti Chic
Madonna di Campiglio, Italy
BARTOLINI\LANZI architects

1   Wooden walls allow flexibility to change
    and stagger shelving

2   Entry is a double volume; the floor is of
    local stone and American walnut wood
    accents add elegance

3   Upper level has staggered hanging systems
    to maximise displays. Mirrors are located
    behind the displays.

4   Men's section at lower level has five steps
    leading to the cash register area. This
    section is constructed entirely of wood

5   Shoes and bags are at the lower level
    where the flooring is of rustic stone. Low
    ceiling is downplayed with boxed lighting
    that maximises levels of illumination.

Photography: Alessandro Bartolini

4

5

TNTBLU
Toronto, Ontario, Canada
Johnson Chou Inc

1   New retail concept for store specialising in denim and casual wear is long and narrow. Dramatic cantilevered cash desk and denim bar suspended from the ceiling articulates the fluidity of the space.
2   Changing rooms are capsules – fluid forms that transform as doors open and close
3   Walls are conceived as blank canvases with light 'painted' onto the walls, floors and ceiling surfaces
Photography: Volker Seding

2

Address Istanbul Shopping & Lifestyle Centre
Istanbul, Turkey
Emre Arolat Architects
1   Dark-coloured ceilings, mirrored floors with recessed pebble beds and black pillars highlight the colours of the storefronts
2   Furniture displays are brought into focus by their soft-coloured backdrops
3   Night view of interior. A luminescent glow surrounds the store displays as the background recedes.
4   Contemporary furniture is displayed on wooden floors and is offset by the mirror-finish floors beyond
Photography: Ilkay Muratoglu

2

3

4

Continental Vision
New York, New York, USA
Studio Gaia

1 Vivid tangerine orange in the feature walls and stools combines with cool white floors and wood veneer furniture in this up-tempo eyewear store

2 Entry is from a busy street. Glass-fronted product displays are recessed and elongated.

3 Innovative lighting makes this store appear larger than it really is

4 Built-in couch saves space. Concealed lighting from within the table recess adds a cosy touch.

5 Cash area is part of the continuous service counter

Photography: Moon Lee Photography

1

2

3

4

5

City Mall
San Pedro Sula, Honduras
Beame Architectural Partnership PA

1   Arrival sequence for valet parking and
     passenger drop-off resembles a five-star
     hotel
2   U-shaped structure has hollow centre
     with internal stepped plaza that
     replicates topography of site
3   Modern interpretations of Eastern details
     such as grillwork, railings and minarets
     and a series of vaulted ceilings are
     special highlights
4   Entire mall is enclosed and air conditioned
     for comfort in the humid, tropical
     environment

Photography: New York Focus

1

3

4

Hetzler Store
Munich, Germany
Gonzalez / Haase Atelier Architecture &
Scenography

1   Space within is conceived as one
    large show window – an effect
    created by a monolithic screen with
    extraordinary material properties that
    generate an ambiguous play with
    spatial limits
2   Store is located within a well-known
    luxury hotel in the heart of Munich.
3   Shop stocks several high-profile
    designer brands
4&5 Mirrors, high-gloss lacquered surfaces,
    carefully articulated nuances of depth
    and monochrome surfaces in dark
    purple create a lively interaction
    between surface structures

Photography: Thomas Meyer/Ostkreuz

1

2

3

4

5

1

2

4

5

3

Vizio Eyewear and Photogallery
Toronto, Ontario, Canada
Johnson Chou Inc

1   Eyewear displays are composed of stainless steel shelves, glass casing and removable protective glass screens
2   Glass and stainless steel are used throughout against neutral white walls
3   Furniture elements slide, tilt and pivot. Two fitting tables are suspended from ceiling tracks and can be repositioned along the length of the store.
4   Store merges two functions that are both well defined and complementary. Eyewear is displayed to the left and a photo gallery is on the right.
5   Tables and seating function as focal points: fitting tables nestle beside a cushioned bench for gallery patrons

Photography: Isaac Applebaum

Bruschi
Bolzano, Italy
BARTOLINI\LANZI architects

1 Marble ground floor has centre and wall displays of antiquated angled brass and glass. Ceiling chandelier emits sounds of nature.
2 Ceiling is constructed of fibreglass tissue. Lighting is half-recessed and is gold in colour.
3 View from entrance; display wall is constructed of straight glass panes
4 Stairway and enclosing walls are of wood and allow views of both levels. Guardrails are constructed of glass.
5 Shoe display is located at basement level. Curved walls are of wood, carpet is a shade of violet and gold-coloured seats are of restored fibreglass resin.

Photography: Alessandro Bartolini

1

2

3

4

5

6

7

8

9

10

Bruschi
Bolzano, Italy
BARTOLINI\LANZI architects

6   Fitting rooms at rear are concealed by antiquated mirrors. Walls are of crystal sheets with grey tissue pressed in between.

7   Display desk is of angled brass and glass

8   High-end sportswear is on first floor. Floor and part of ceiling are of Italian walnut with recessed lighting on ceiling.

9   Ellipse-shaped lighting is pale and opalescent. Gold-coloured mannequins are of fibreglass.

10   Unisex clothing department is on second floor. Walnut flooring and walls are layered fibreglass and glass and ceiling lights are recessed with inbuilt speakers.

Photography: Alessandro Bartolini

1

2

3

4

AM2
Berlin, Germany
Gonzales / Haase Atelier
Architecture & Scenography

1   Store is located in a hidden Berlin courtyard

2–4 With an environment that is functional and dedicated to a formal process, the store transcends the borders between architecture, scenography and visual art

5   Monochrome, standardised blue accentuates the monumental qualities of furniture

6   Furniture appears as a minimalist object against a backdrop of neutral white

Photography: Thomas Meyer/Ostkreuz

5

6

1

2

3

4

Forum Rio
Ipanema, Rio de Janeiro, Brazil
Isay Weinfeld

1 Strong Brazilian accents are expressed in the architecture of this contemporary fashion store
2 Detail of store window
3 View of first floor with furniture produced by young designers from the Favela da Maré
4 Ground-floor interior
5 View from within store towards window display

Photography: Alvaro Póvoa

5

TNT Woman 2000
Toronto, Ontario, Canada
Johnson Chou Inc

1 Located in Hazelton Lanes, an exclusive shopping mall in the upscale Yorkville District, new store is an expansion to an existing one

2 Composed of acid-etched glass, the translucent screens enclose freestanding display racks offering hazy impressions of the clothing within

3 With its dramatically composed lighting, white walls and translucent glass screens, is a serene, ethereal space

4 Translucent glass screens define the four different boutiques that are set 3 metres apart to create individual rooms. Adjacent to the screens are adjustable custom-designed display racks that are recessed into drywall alcoves.

Photography: Volker Seding

1

2

3

4

1

2

TNT Woman 2001
Toronto, Ontario, Canada
Johnson Chou Inc

1   Space is distinguished by two main elements that define movement through the store: four frame-like steel structures that display merchandise and a large, circular cash desk clad in stainless steel

2   Store features custom-designed display fixtures that are adjustable in various configurations

3   Ethereal design of fitting rooms is intended to inspire a memorable experience for boutique's customers

Photography: Volker Seding

3

1

2

3

4

5

Clemensborg
Århus, Denmark
schmidt hammer lassen k/s

1   Dynamic dialogue between existing historic brick building and modern transparent extension of steel and glass is visible in the grandeur of its fine façade
2   Oval atrium permits natural light to filter down through the floors and is the interface between the old and the new
3   Easily accessible system of escalators and lifts connects the internal shopping centre floors
4   Clemensborg bridge connects with the Århus Aa River promenade, giving easy access to shoppers
5   Sleek interiors within the gracious historic building skilfully blend the present with its past

Photography: Sølvbjærg Fotografi

The MIXC at City Crossing
Shenzen, Guangdong Province, China
RTKL Associates Inc

1   Building envelope comprises diverse architectural forms. Horizontal massing of the centre is balanced with the 32-storey office tower.
2   Centre features a multi-level public open space system
3   Glass curtain walls offer striking views into and out of the centre
4   Centre is strongly linked to the surrounding urban context
5   Retail centre has an atypical vertical configuration

Photography: Tim Griffith

2

3

4

5

1

2

3

Ostbahnhof
East Berlin, Germany
Becker Gewers Kühn + Kühn

1   Generous entrance area is marked by
    wide transparent overlapping roof. An
    all-glass façade opens the station up
    towards the city like a huge shop display
    window.

2   Escalators, galleries and information
    pavilions are dynamically displayed.
    Filtered daylight shines though a
    seemingly weightless roof of steel
    and glass.

3   Building, which had been converted
    during GDR regime was dark, opaque and
    confusing. Modernised to true 21st-
    century style, it is today a bright place
    of urban mobility.

Photography: Jens Willebrand & Claus Graubner

1

2

Mitsubishi Trust Financial Group & UFJ Bank Private Banking Office
Nagoya, Japan
Neil M. Denari Architects Inc

1   Black metal façade installed over existing 1970's office building reflects Japanese aesthetics
2   Laser-cut patterns forms screen for second-floor windows and imparts a modern look
3   Subtle curvatures and angles of the surfaces are specially designed to create welcoming space
4   Main reception hall is a space of transition where reception and small conference rooms are shaped by smooth surfaces of wood
5   Mimicking fine Japanese lacquered bowls, interior of bank is in stark contrast to colours and material inside the Quick Corner ATM Hall and Private Banking Office on first floor

Photography: Neil M. Denari

3

4

5

**Mitsubishi Trust Financial Group & UFJ
Bank Private Banking Office
Nagoya, Japan**
Neil M. Denari Architects Inc

6   Smooth surfaces that shape ceilings
    and walls, contrasting materials of
    white plaster and two types of wood
    veneer combine in a unique manner to
    set this interior design apart

7–9 Furniture and walls appear to be
    suspended. The design features also
    create curiosity among the bank
    customers, reflecting MUFG's
    innovative approach to clients.

Photography: Neil M. Denari

6

8

GREED
Osaka, Japan
Area Design

1 Cool and quiet interior of store has an atmosphere of subtle elegance
2 Night view of discreet entrance with illuminated display window
Photography: Shimomura Photo Office

2

Best Point
Norwood, South Australia, Australia
Studio 9 Architects Pty Ltd

1 Design concept for retail paving/stone
   showroom space creates 'end vision'
   of what pavers look like when installed

2 Passersby are drawn to store both day
   and night by an illuminated 'Red Wall'

3 Fitout achieves more visual 'punch'
   through retaining colours, spaces
   and forms

4&5 Interactive displays where tiles/pavers
     can be touched and visualised

Photography: Sarah Long Photography

3

4

FILA Madison Avenue
New York, New York, USA
Giorgio Borruso Design

1   Sense of movement projects through transparent exterior
    of this sports company's flagship store
2   Evoking a course in the air, the design suggests a path to
    move through fixtures
3   Two ellipsoidal metallic elements envelop existing columns
    in middle of store space. Display furniture resembles
    muscles in tension, ready at any moment to spring to life.

Photography: Benny Chan

1

4   Dramatic shoe display design is reminiscent of birds in flight along a canted wall textured with delicate waves

Photography: Benny Chan

…ina è un capolavoro di ingegneria ed un' opera d'arte. – Leonardo da Vinci

FILA Madison Avenue
New York, New York, USA
Giorgio Borruso & Associates

5   Curvilinear elements wrapping the existing columns in the middle of store appear to descend from ceiling in search of an anchor

6&7   Movement is omnipresent in the décor, with expressions of lightness and grace evident in the fixtures

Photography: Benny Chan

6

7

Desert Ridge Marketplace
Phoenix, Arizona, USA
MCG Architecture

1   This centre responds to the community's demand for varying retail facilities in one location. In contrast to the area's Southwestern style, the marketplace uses an American architectural palette of earth colours, stone and wood finishes.

2   Open-air project integrates six distinctive shopping districts consisting of home improvement, fashion, restaurants, entertainment/lifestyle, home design and neighbourhood convenience

3   Centre offers the excitement of a dynamic destination retail centre in a humanistic style and scale

4   Shutters, canopies, covered walkways and shed roofs with skylights distinguish the project

Photography: Lansing Photography

2

3

4

Snaidero Showroom
Los Angeles, California, USA
Giorgio Borruso Design

1   Renowned Italian kitchen and design company Snaidero adopted a unique contemporary design approach for its new showroom. White ribbons spiral upwards, wrapping around to converge and transform into the projecting mezzanine. Modern accent speakers add interest.
2   Circular 'Acropolis' designed by Pininfarina is overhung by and nearly sucked into the white ascending spiral
3   Design utilised existing building with uninteresting façade but large bay windows by downplaying the exterior and highlighting the interior
4   Stairway leading to mezzanine is completely exposed. Suspended by aircraft cable and finished in dark oak, it is a continuation of the floor.

Photography: Benny Chan

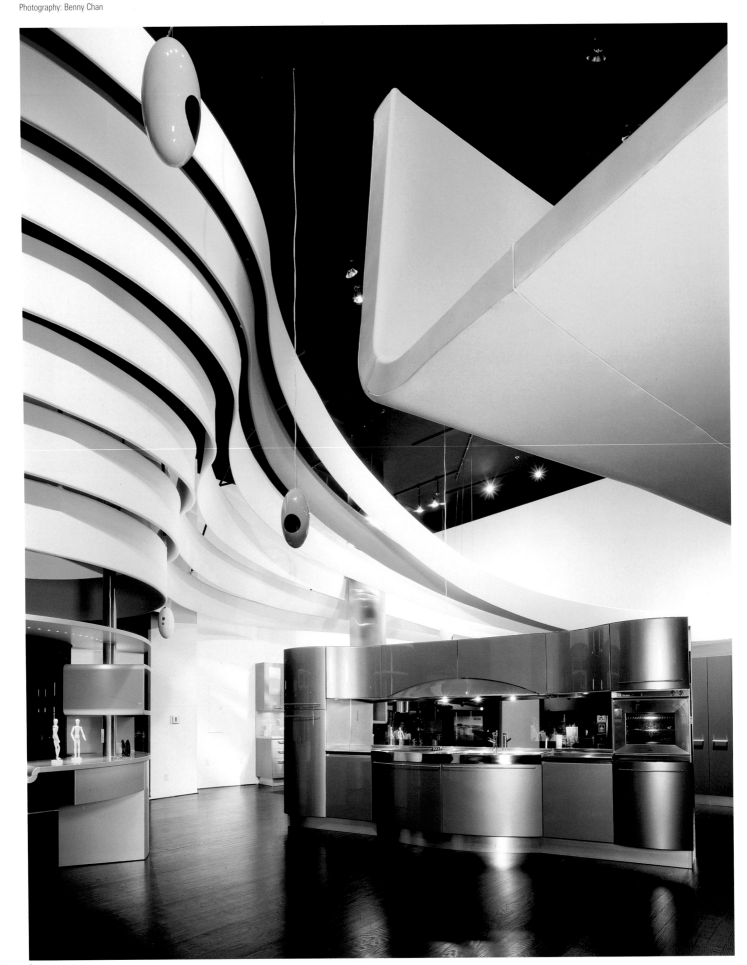

2

3

4

2

3

4

Fornarina Mandalay Bay
Las Vegas, Nevada, USA
Giorgio Borruso Design

1   The design concept was to create an oasis within the bustle of Mandalay Bay

2   The store is composed of a sophisticated system of integrated 'organs'. The visitor is invited inside and exposed to a range of beautiful products.

3&4   Pearlescent and chrome fibreglass rings, embedded in suspended resin panels with delicate waves, display shoes and accessories

5   Four large lighting elements made of aluminium wrapped in a membrane of fabric and PVC hang from the ceiling in the middle of the store

Photography: Benny Chan

5

6   Cascading resin panels are pierced with pearlescent and chrome fibreglass display rings.
     Floor undulations are custom-made vinyl and contain tiny flecks of colour.
7   Hanging light elements pulsate with Fornarina's signature rhodamine-red colour

Photography: Benny Chan

2

Marketplace @ Centerra
Loveland, Colorado, USA
MCG Architecture
1   Design of centre embodies the Rocky Mountains through the use of stone, metal and trellis elements
2&3   Two of the many restaurants and cafés located throughout the centre
Photography: Architectural Photography Inc

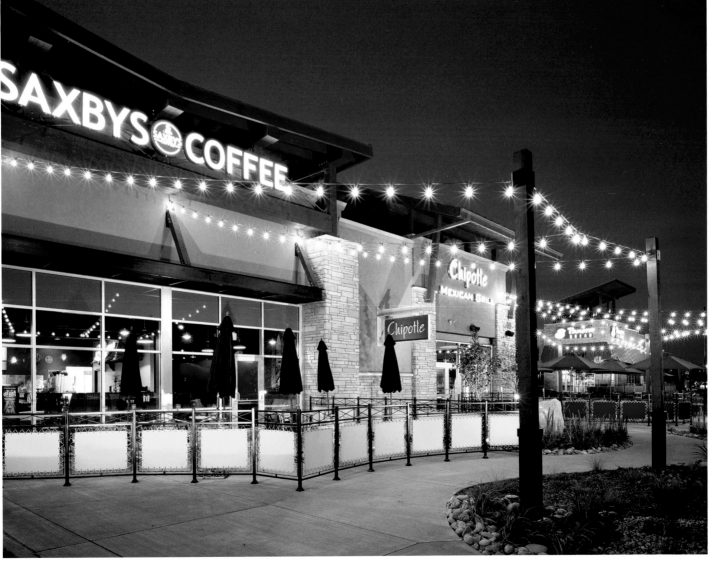

3

Marketplace @ Centerra
Loveland, Colorado, USA
MCG Architecture
   4   Daytime view of Chipotle Mexican Grill
5&6   Two well-known fashion retailers are tenants in the centre
Photography: Architectural Photography Inc

5

6

1

2

3

4

5

Dolphin Mall
Miami, Florida, USA
Beame Architectural Partnership, PA

1&4 Open-air entertainment plaza with a bookstore and cafés flanks main mall entry and serves as a grand entrance

2 Megamall features a 'racetrack' public circulation plan intersected by high-presentation retail

3&6 Many entertainment retailers are strategically placed to anchor other areas, including a food court with a kids' play area

5 Filigree-like designs on arches form part of the design elements of the interior

7 Value retail and specialty shops, family entertainment, a cinemaplex, bowling alley, dining and parking for more than 7,000 cars are among the many features of this mall

Photography: Thomas Delbeck Photography (1,2,7); Dan Forer (3–6)

6

7

Kinshicho
Tokyo, Japan
RTKL Associates Inc

1 Retail corridors are lined with a series of whimsical environmental graphics
2 Various architectural forms highlight main entryways
3 Exterior architecture links to the surrounding urban context
4 Interior circulation offers multiple-level visibility
Photography: Nacasa and Partners

1

2

3

1

2

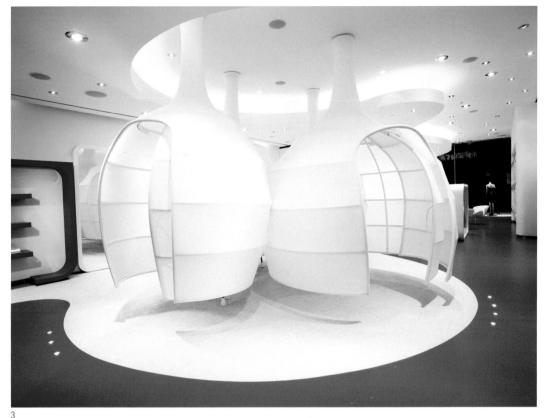

3

Miss Sixty
Aventura, Florida, USA
Giorgio Borruso Design

1   Product displays of shoes and accessories are sleek
    and uncluttered. Comfortable seating is provided.

2   The approach to the store is an oversized metal
    sculptural element, surrounded by glass. The
    stainless steel polished mirror door has 12 conical
    portholes.

3   Suspended cocoon-shaped dressing rooms made
    of special ultra-light aluminium circles surrounded
    with tensile translucent fabric have a distinct
    avant-garde feel

4   The cash counter is virtually seamless, curving in two
    directions. It reveals a background of red glass that is
    retro-illuminated with hypnotic shadowy disks.

Photography: Benny Chan

4

1

2

3

Mt. Shasta Mall
Redding, California, USA
MCG Architecture

1   Ageing centre was renovated to include a new identity programme that introduced an ambience of creativity and life
2   Food court
3   In-line shops and pedestrian corridors were replaced with a new curvilinear design that includes pedestrian living rooms and festive plazas
4   Entry
5   Pedestrian living room
Photography: Whittaker Photography

4

5

Bruuns Galleri
Århus, Denmark
schmidt hammer lassen k/s

1   Situated in the heart of Århus, adjacent
    to the bridge M.P. Bruuns Bro and Århus
    Central Station, the centre contains
    shops, cafes, restaurants and cinemas

2   Architecturally, the centre exemplifies
    industrial chic. Transparent façades offer
    deep vistas into the complex.

Opposite:
    The KPMG Building located nearby
    assures a unique synergistic relationship
    with central Århus and the city
    infrastructure

Photography: Sølvbjærg Fotografi

1

2

The 49 Terrace
Bangkok, Thailand
A49

1   Street entrance surrounded by retail shops and spaces for relaxing
2   Street façade at night. Starbucks Coffee is located on ground floor
3   Central courtyard space links all retail levels

Photography: Wison Tungthunya

1

2

3

1   Cashwrap sweeps upward from floor in a succession of curves like a wave crashing into the space
2   Transparent façade of store invites the visitor inside
3   Colourful display racks encourage interaction as they slide out to reveal additional displays behind,
    allowing a continually changing configuration of colours
Photography: Benny Chan

2

3

4   Display wall has interchangeable system for display, communication, shelves, casework, to leave personal notes or even mount a bicycle
5   Display wall has added depth with unique shelves that pull out to access hidden storage
6   Douglas fir wall is a display for many objects, including a surfboard
Photography: Benny Chan

5

6

1

2

3

QueensPlaza
Brisbane, Queensland, Australia
PDT Architects in association with RTKL Architects/Los Angeles, USA
1   Night view of plaza on Queen and Edward Street corner
2   View of three floors with dome on upper level
3   View of three floors with food court on lower ground floor
4   Ground floor entry from Queen Street
Photography: Aperture Architectural Photography

QueensPlaza
Brisbane, Queensland, Australia
PDT Architects in association with RTKL
Architects/Los Angeles, USA
5   Ground-floor retail space
6   First-floor café overlooking Queen Street mall
7   Some of the elegant shops on ground floor
Photography: Aperture Architectural Photography

6

7

Multiplaza Pacific
Panama City, Panama
RTKL Associates Inc

1   Columns towering above the roof position the centre as a highly visible landmark
2   Streamlined scheme lends a sense of identity to individual tenants
3   Interior is designed to resemble a streetscape
4   Dining and entertainment options are closely integrated with retail tenants

Photography: David Whitcomb

1

2

3

1

2

3

4

Habitat & Nike Stores
Monte Carlo, Monaco
Mellett Architects

1 Nike 'place' within the 'New House of Light' adapted itself to the rehabilitated Saint Charles food market. A great semi-urban black glass archway links Monte Carlo with the world of Nike.

2&3 Store defines itself as a 'Nike architectural experience' between urban shop and loft space

4 Two giant vitrines flank the main entrance to Habitat's New Generation of stores

5&6 Forty years after opening its first store in London, Habitat Monte Carlo celebrates the Monaco Habitat store

Photography: courtesy Mellett Architects

5

6

7

8

Habitat Stores
Monte Carlo, Monaco
Mellett Architects

7&8 The store is on three levels and the
entry is oriented towards the 'Place'
in front of Saint Charles Church

9–11 Habitat's trademark furniture and
homewares are displayed in a
marked Monegasque style

Photography: courtesy Mellett Architects

9

Principe Pio
Madrid, Spain
RTKL Associates Inc

1   Centre is located in the heart of Madrid's historic area
2   Expansive glass canopy links new retail centre with an existing train station
Opposite:
     Retail design promotes fluid circulation
Photography: David Whitcomb

1

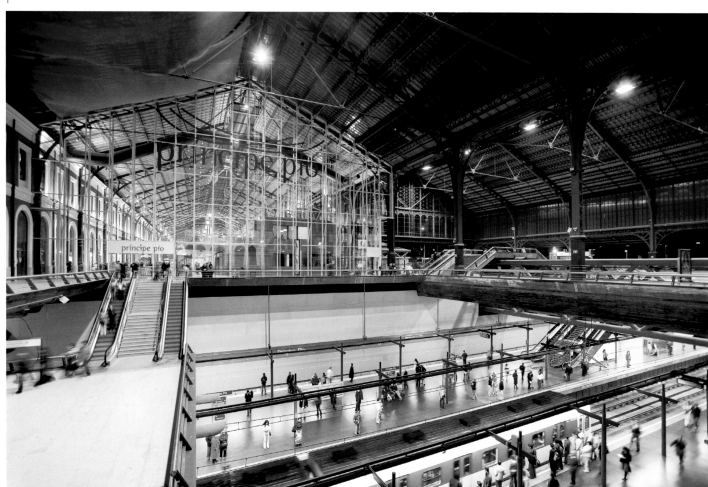

2

4

5

6

4   Centre includes diverse dining options
5   Scheme includes sunken level of retail
6   Dining terrace overlooks retail levels
7   Retail and transit uses seamlessly coexist
Photography: David Whitcomb

7

1

Terramall
San Jose, Costa Rica
Beame Architectural Partnership PA

1   Food court is one of the many facilities offered; others include fashion retailers, a supermarket, cinemaplex, music court, restaurants and more than 200 shops
2   Covered walkways offer convenient access during the rainy season
3   Three-level plan responds to sloping site and creates at-grade customer entrances from parking fields at all levels

Photography: Thomas Delbeck Photography

2

3

Terramall
San Jose, Costa Rica
Beame Architectural Partnership PA

4   Retail shops overlook food court
5   Cinemaplex in centre offers a variety of entertainment
6&7   Open-air common areas are designed to harness natural
      breezes and preserve views of surrounding mountains
Photography: Thomas Delbeck Photography

4

5

6

7

Fornarina Via Dei Condotti
Rome, Italy
Giorgio Borruso Design

1 This established Italian retailer of women's fashion, shoes and accessories is located inside a 16th-century building on the Via Dei Condotti, one of the world's most fashionable areas

2 From the outside, the dramatic view includes elegant fashion displays

3 From the entrance, a wall composed of black lacquer panels with a series of embedded 'eyes' is visible. The eyes flirtatiously hinge open and shut to display shoes and accessories and also change colour alternating between white and rhodamine red.

4 Three pearlescent-white, tall panels perforated by chrome rings are suspended and run the full height between the two floors

5 Floor has curves of white vinyl and black resin that flow through the space like a fluid, encouraging shoppers to move throughout the levels

Photography: Benny Chan

1

2

3

4

1

Cassis
Toronto, Ontario, Canada
II BY IV Design Associates Inc

1   As an unusual design feature, half the
    storefront is devoted to a stylish and
    welcoming foyer. The other half of the
    storefront has a metal structure; soft drapery
    frames view into the store interior.

2   Deeply textured upholstery in autumnal tones
    covers the wardrobe lounge armchairs, change
    room seats and display benches. Metal
    elements are in soft-toned brass finish.

3   Cove lighting, recessed spot lights, perimeter
    uplighting, halo-lit mirrors and residential-like
    floor, table and pendant lamps fill the space
    with a soft and ambient glow

4   Mannequins stand on runway down length of
    store providing visual landmarks and wardrobe
    inspiration

Photography: Evan Dion Photographer Inc

2

3

4

NikeWomen Fashion Island
Newport Beach, California, USA
BOORA Architects with Brand Design, Nike, Inc

1   Overall design inspiration derives from Palm Springs Modern structures of the 1950s
2   Aluminium storefront system and stacked 'stone' wall made of recycled fibreboard
3   Blue glass mosaic tile 'welcome mat' draws customers into store from entry. The
    welcome mat culminates in a display of featured apparel, echoing a fashion runway.

Photography: Craig Dugan at Hedrich Blessing

2

3

NikeWomen Fashion Island
Newport Beach, California, USA
BOORA Architects with Brand Design, Nike, Inc

4   A calm, elegant boutique, residential in scale and character
5   Residential accessories such as vases, framed pictures and wood cases
     contribute to the feel of the store
6   Sustainably harvested hardwood floors add rich texture to the space
7   Blue glass 'welcome mat' is a novel way to invite customers into the store
Photography: Craig Dugan at Hedrich Blessing

4

5

6

1

2

Westfield Century City
Los Angeles, California, USA
Rios Clementi Hale Studios in association with Westfield Corporation

1&2   Dining terrace spills casually into the outdoors, acting as a central gathering and eating area. The adjacent newstand is designed by Corsini Architects with guidelines by Rios Clementi Hale Studios.

3   A large range of products displayed by many well-known brand retailers

Photography: Tom Bonner Photography

3

4

6

5

Westfield Century City
Los Angeles, California, USA
Rios Clementi Hale Studios in association with Westfield Corporation

4   Outdoor dining terrace

5   A highly collaborative design process created a contemporary urban shopping centre that reflects the mall's sophisticated customer base. It added a new second level with an indoor/outdoor dining terrace.

6   Indoor dining terrace offers a refined experience achieved through modern furnishings and planters and real dishware provided by notNeutral – the homeware product line of the architect

Photography: Tom Bonner Photography

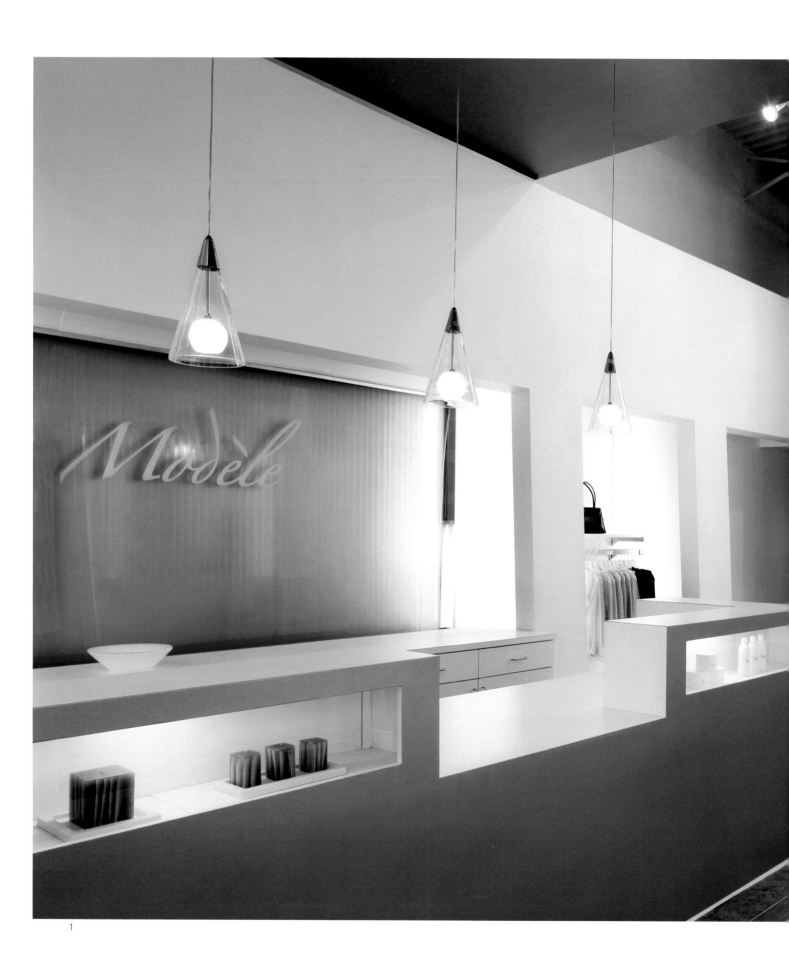

1

2

Modèle
Omaha, Nebraska, USA
Randy Brown Architects

1　Sleek backdrop lends itself perfectly for the 'hip' merchandise.
　　Store was designed to have a Soho (New York) flavour.

2　Unfinished concrete floors, exposed ceilings and geometric lines
　　create a minimal look on an affordable budget

Photography: Farshid Assassi

Modèle
Omaha, Nebraska, USA
Randy Brown Architects

Opposite:
    Display areas are dramatic and
    maximise clothing display
4   Clean lines and 'cut-out' design are
    tailor-made for a fashion store
5   Open and spacious, the boutique is yet
    inviting and welcoming

Photography: Farshid Assassi

1

3

2

Kitson Men
Los Angeles, California, USA
Space International Inc

1   Kitson Men store evolved from the hugely successful Kitson and Kitson Kids stores and retails a wide range of high-end brands
2   Displays of toiletries, accessories and clothing jostle for space along the interesting display wall
3&5 Store is off a busy Hollywood street
4   Captured glimpses of the landscaped courtyard adjacent to the retail area offer a sense of calm and stillness

Photography: Joshua White

4

5

6

7

8

Kitson Men
Los Angeles, California, USA
Space International Inc
6   Storefront displays form a connection between retail and pedestrian spaces
7   Translucent-fronted changing rooms are fabricated steel boxes along the popular Robertson Boulevard shopping street
8   Inside, walls and ceilings of a portion of the store are clad in plywood panels that take on the effect of stippled sunlight
     through a canopy of trees
Photography: Joshua White

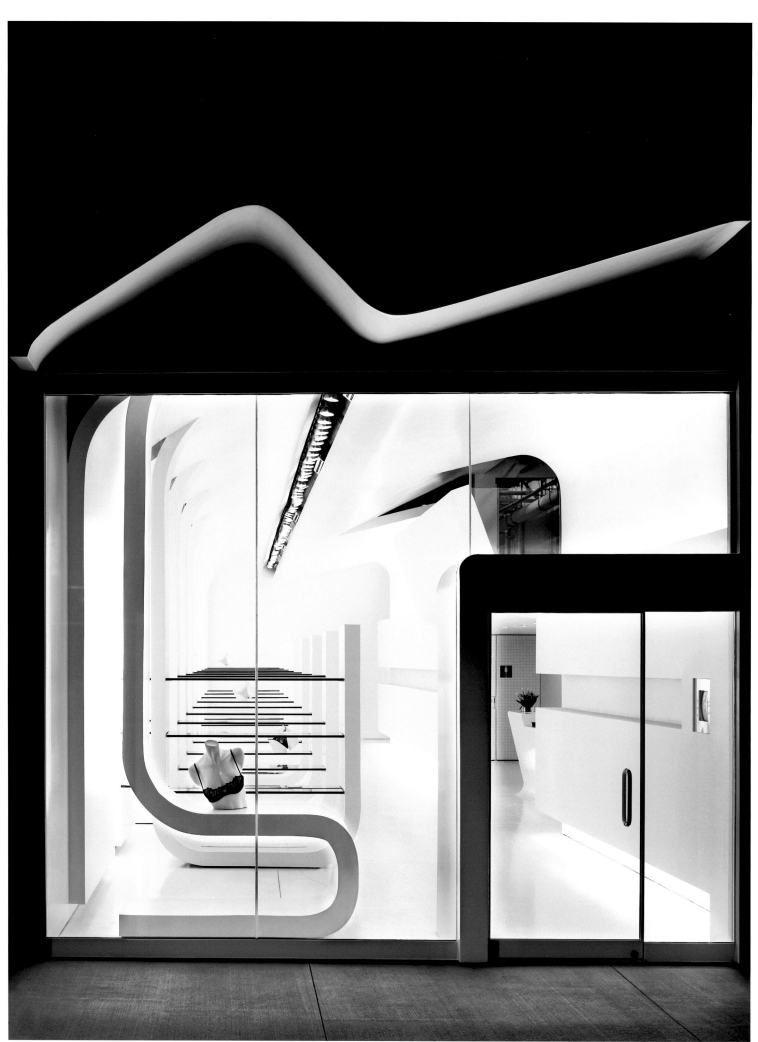

Bizarre
Omaha, Nebraska, USA
Randy Brown Architect

1 Inspired by folds of paper, interior was designed to be light, bright and simple to best show off merchandise
2 Cash wrap is a sleek angled counter that enhances the minimalist image of the store
3 Unique lingerie displays against innovatively lit wall
4 Based around a series of 'pods', the space is almost transparent and has a distinctive lightness that enables the merchandise to 'float'

Photography: Fashid Assassi

2

3

4

Bizarre
Omaha, Nebraska, USA
Randy Brown Architect

5   Sophisticated illumination from floor
level and above bathes the store in an
ethereal glow

6&7   Displays are modern and minimalist

8   View from above into the pod-like
design elements

Photography: Farshid Assassi

6

7

8

NikeTown
New York, New York, USA
BOORA Architects in association with Brand Designs Nike, Inc
1   Open display window allows views to ground-floor retail space
2   Sleek entry lobby offers a suggestion of streamlined shopping experience within
3   A light 'cloud' in the ceiling adds interest to the eyewear sales corner
4   Nike's much-recognised yet understated logo adorns a prominent wall
Photography: Peter Mauss/Esto for Nike Inc

2

3

5

6

5   Lighting 'clouds', updated displays and increased connections between spaces improve the feeling of openness and accessibility throughout the store
6   Wood flooring and exposed ceiling structure in the upper level of store add rich texture
7   Free-standing displays, targeted illumination and exposed ceiling structure all add a touch of chic to the store

Photography: Peter Mauss/Esto for Nike Inc

NikeTown
New York, New York, USA
BOORA Architects in association with Brand Designs Nike, Inc

8   The Nike brand is given ideal exposure in this design where movement and stillness combine

9&10   Modern displays with simple lines focus attention to apparel line

Photography: Peter Mauss/Esto for Nike Inc

9

INDEX OF ARCHITECTS

ACKNOWLEDGEMENTS

We are grateful to all the participating architects, architecture firms and designers whose work is featured in this publication. We also acknowledge the invaluable contribution of the photographers who, so willingly, submitted their brilliant work. Without their cooperation, this publication would not be a reality